Mon and the Red Frog

By Sally Cowan

Mon and Mum got
fresh crabs from the mud.

"Crabs are too little,"
said Mon.
"I am **very** hungry!"

"Let's look for frogs up here," said Mum.
"Fresh frogs will fill you up!"

Mon went for a frog,
but it got away from him.

Hop, hop, hop!

"Be quick, Mon!" said Mum.

Then, Mon looked at
a red frog with black dots.

It looked yum!

Mon got the frog!

The hot sun hit the frog.

It had wet froth on it.

Stop, Mon! Red frogs are very bad for us!

Mon got a big shock!

He let the red frog go.

Off it went, with a big hop!

Get **that** frog, Mon.
It's **not** red with black dots!

This fresh frog is good!

CHECKING FOR MEANING

1. How was Mon feeling at the start of the story? *(Literal)*

2. What colour was the first frog Mon found? *(Literal)*

3. What might have happened if Mon had eaten the red frog? *(Inferential)*

EXTENDING VOCABULARY

fresh	What does it mean if the crabs in the story are *fresh*?
froth	What does *froth* mean? What is another word that has a similar meaning and could have been used in this story? I.e. bubbles.
Stop	Why did Mum use this word? Why was she warning Mon? Which word can be used as the opposite of *stop* and begins with *st*–? I.e. start.

MOVING BEYOND THE TEXT

1. How do young animals learn what foods are suitable to eat? Who teaches them how to catch or hunt for food?

2. What fresh foods do you most like to eat? Why?

3. What can we do to help keep our food fresh?

4. Where can we find foods to eat other than the supermarket or markets? Are these foods safe for us to eat?

SPEED SOUNDS

bl	gl	cr	fr	st

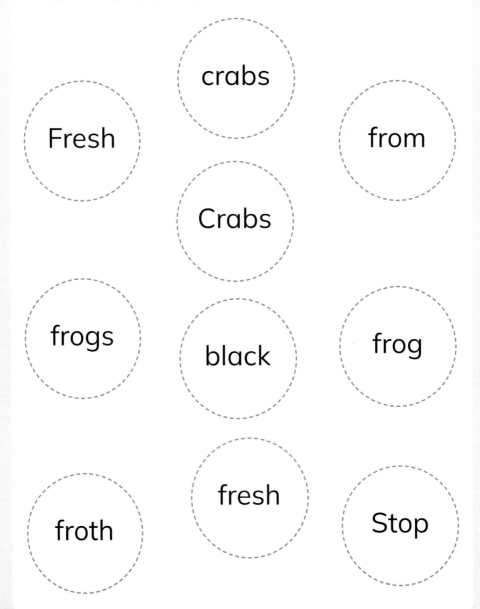

crabs

Fresh

from

Crabs

frogs

black

frog

froth

fresh

Stop